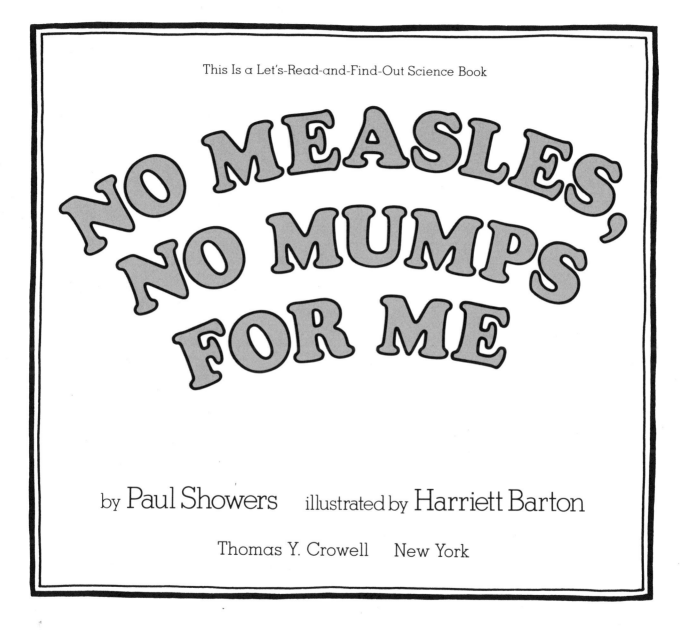

This Is a Let's-Read-and-Find-Out Science Book

NO MEASLES, NO MUMPS FOR ME

by Paul Showers   illustrated by Harriett Barton

Thomas Y. Crowell   New York

OTHER *Let's-Read-and-Find-Out Science Books* YOU WILL ENJOY

A Baby Starts to Grow by Paul Showers • *Before You Were a Baby* by Paul Showers and Kay Sperry Showers • *A Drop of Blood* by Paul Showers • *Fat and Skinny* by Philip Balestrino • *Hear Your Heart* by Paul Showers • *How Many Teeth?* by Paul Showers • *How You Talk* by Paul Showers • *Look at Your Eyes* by Paul Showers • *Me and My Family Tree* by Paul Showers • *The Skeleton Inside You* by Philip Balestrino • *Straight Hair, Curly Hair* by Augusta Goldin • *Use Your Brain* by Paul Showers • *Your Skin and Mine* by Paul Showers

Let's-Read-and-Find-Out Science Books are edited by Dr. Roma Gans, Professor Emeritus of Childhood Education, Teachers College, Columbia University, and Dr. Franklyn M. Branley, Astronomer Emeritus and former Chairman of The American Museum-Hayden Planetarium. For a complete catalog of *Let's-Read-and-Find-Out Science Books,* write to Thomas Y. Crowell, Department 363, 10 East 53rd Street, New York, New York 10022.

I like to hear my grandmother tell stories. I like the stories about when she was a little girl. My grandmother was sick a lot when she was little.

First she got whooping cough. She coughed all day and all night. Sometimes she had trouble catching her breath. She had to go to bed and stay there.

Grandmother got over whooping cough. Later she got the mumps. Her face swelled up on both sides. It hurt her to chew and swallow. Pickles hurt her the most. She couldn't eat them at all.

Grandmother got over the mumps. Later she got the measles. She had a fever and a runny nose. There were red spots all over her body. She had to go to bed with the measles, too.

I'm glad I didn't live in those days. Children
got whooping cough, measles, and mumps. They

got rubella, polio, tetanus, and diphtheria. Some children got very sick. Some even died.

I've never had whooping cough or mumps or measles or polio or any of the rest. And I never will, either. Because I've had shots, and sometimes special drops.

When you get the shots, or the drops, you are helping your body to keep well. This is how your body does it.

Inside your body, the blood is always moving. It moves through arteries and veins. It moves to every part of you—up to your head, out to your arms and hands, down to your legs and feet.

Many tiny cells are carried by your blood. They are so small you need a microscope to see them.

Under a microscope you can see fat, round, red cells. There are millions of them. Here and there, you can see white cells, too. The white cells are bigger than the red cells.

There are different kinds of white cells in your body. They are in your blood, and in other parts of you, too.

The white cells in your body help to keep you well. They fight germs and kill them.

Not all germs make you sick, but some do. Germs called viruses can give you polio, measles, mumps, and rubella.

Germs called bacteria can give you diphtheria, whooping cough, and tetanus.

There are many different kinds of viruses. They are so small you need a powerful microscope to see them.

Bacteria are bigger than viruses, but you still need a microscope to see them. Some bacteria are round and grow in clusters. Some are long and thin like rods. Others are shaped like little spirals.

rod-shaped bacteria

16

Bacteria and viruses get into your body in
many ways. They enter through cuts in your skin,
through your mouth, or through your nose when
you breathe.

When bacteria get inside your body, each one splits into two. Each of these new bacteria splits again and again and again. Viruses grow even faster. When a virus gets inside your body, it turns into hundreds of viruses all at once. Each of these viruses then turns into many more viruses.

Once bacteria or viruses get inside your body, there will soon be millions and millions more just like them. Unless something fights them, you may get very sick.

White cells in your body fight the germs. They fight them in many ways. When I had my shot for whooping cough, this is how they worked.

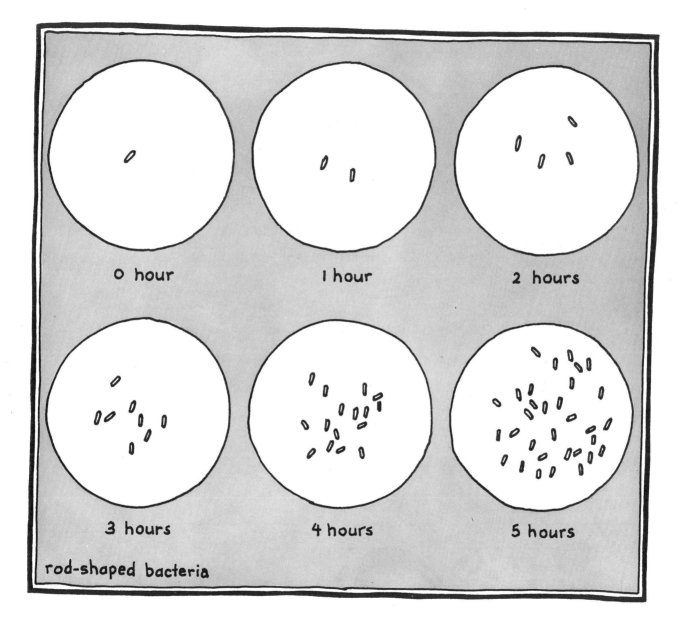

O hour 1 hour 2 hours

3 hours 4 hours 5 hours

rod-shaped bacteria

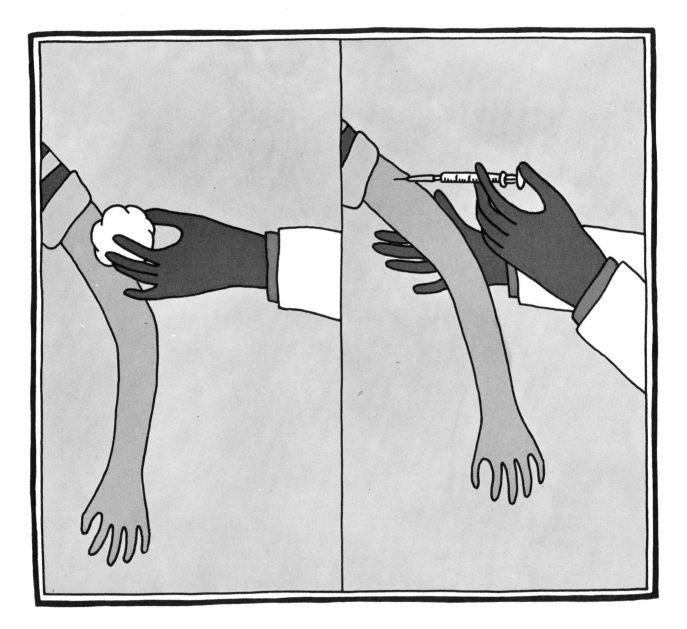

First, the doctor rubbed my arm with alcohol to clean it. That made my arm feel cool. Then the doctor stuck the needle in my arm. It hurt a little, but only for a few seconds. I didn't mind. I knew what would happen inside me.

The needle was full of whooping-cough germs. They were weak germs. They were too weak to harm me.

The germs were like a signal. Soon some of my white cells swelled up. They started making a chemical to kill the whooping-cough germs. The chemical is called an antibody—anti means against. An antibody is a chemical that fights germs.

The antibodies poured into my blood. They were carried to my arms and hands, my feet and legs, to every part of me. Soon they had killed all the weak germs from my whooping-cough shot. I never felt a thing. Some kids feel a little sick after a shot, but I didn't.

The antibodies are still in my blood. They are ready to fight any whooping-cough germs that get inside my body.

Whooping-cough germs are bacteria. Polio germs are different. They are viruses. The other day I went to the doctor to get the special drops. Weak polio germs were in those drops. My doctor gave them to me on a sugar cube.

When I swallowed the drops, a different kind of white cell went to work inside me. This kind is sometimes called a killer cell. Killer cells fight viruses.

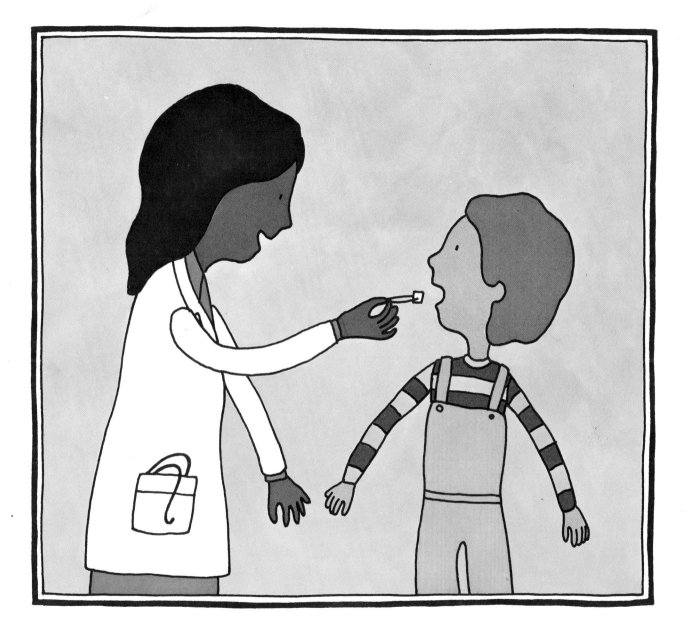

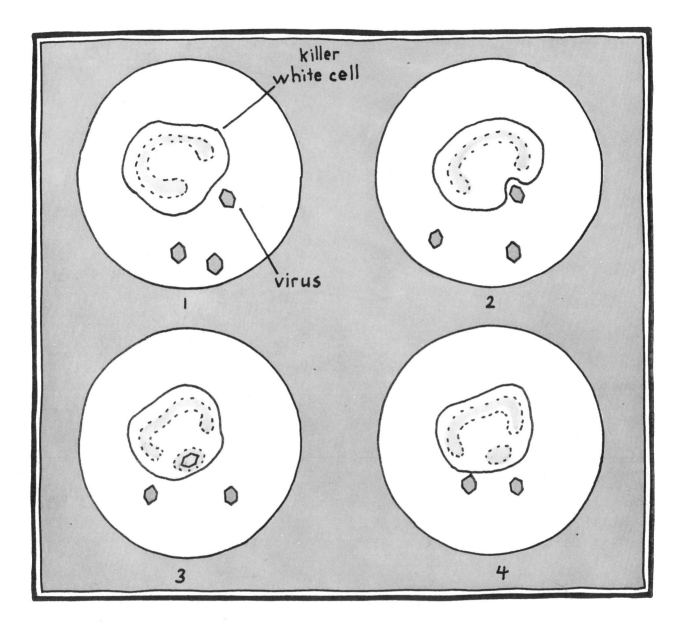

When my killer white cells found the weak germs from the drops, they killed the germs. After that, my killer cells went on looking for more polio germs. They are still looking.

The shots and the special drops I take are like fire drills. A fire drill gets you ready for a real fire. A shot gets you ready for a real attack by strong germs.

Because I've had the shots, and the drops, I will never get sick the way my grandmother did when she was a little girl. I will never get whooping cough or tetanus or diphtheria. My blood is full of antibodies to fight these diseases.

And I will never get polio or measles or mumps or rubella. Killer cells are moving about in my body, day and night. They are ready to wipe out the germs that cause these diseases.

I am immune to whooping cough, polio, and all the rest. That means I can't catch these diseases.

I don't remember getting most of the shots, or the first time I got drops, either. That's because I had them when I was a baby. But once in a while, I still get them. Booster shots and booster drops keep my white cells on the job.

I know all these things because my grandmother told me about them. My grandmother knows a lot.

About the Author

Paul Showers is a retired newspaperman and the author of nearly two dozen books for children. He first became interested in writing for young readers after having watched his own children struggle with the "See, Sally, see" books of the 1950s. His own works—most of them in the Let's-Read-and-Find-Out series—consistently reflect his belief that children's books can be both lively and worthwhile.

Mr. Showers has worked on the Detroit *Free Press,* the New York *Herald Tribune,* the New York *Sunday Mirror,* and, for twenty-nine years, on the Sunday *New York Times.* He was born in Sunnyside, Washington, and was graduated from the University of Michigan, where he received an A.B. degree.

About the Illustrator

Harriett Barton was born in Picher, Oklahoma, and grew up in nearby Miami. A graduate of the University of Kansas, she presently lives in New York City, where she works as a designer of children's books.

614.4 Showers, Paul
S
    No measles, no mumps
    for me

DATE			
OCT 2 5 1982	NOV 2 6 '86		
JAN 2 9 1982			
FEB 1 7 1982	MAR 1 0 1983		
FEB 2 6 1982			
5 MAR 7	MAR 2 1		
MAR 8 8 1982	NOV 2 0	OCT 0 9 1990	
APR 2 8	JAN 2 0		
APR 2 0 198	JAN 2 0		
MAY 4 1982			
MAY 2 5 1982			
NOV 1 8 1982			
MAY 2 1			